The Lost Cow

Mara Bergman • Jonatronix

OXFORD
UNIVERSITY PRESS

Molly

Farm

manure

Molly has a farm.

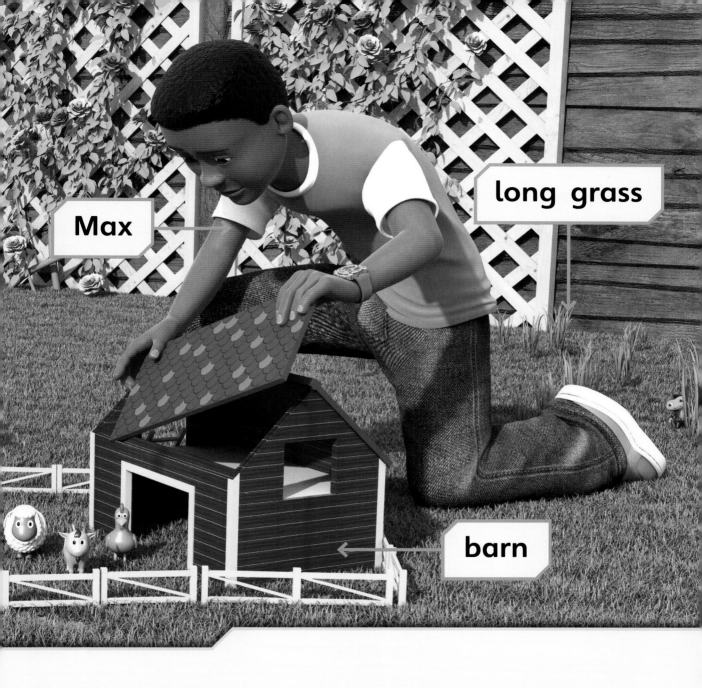

Max

long grass

barn

It has a sheep, a goat and a hen.

Molly looks for her cow.
It is missing.

Max thinks he can help.

Max shrinks.

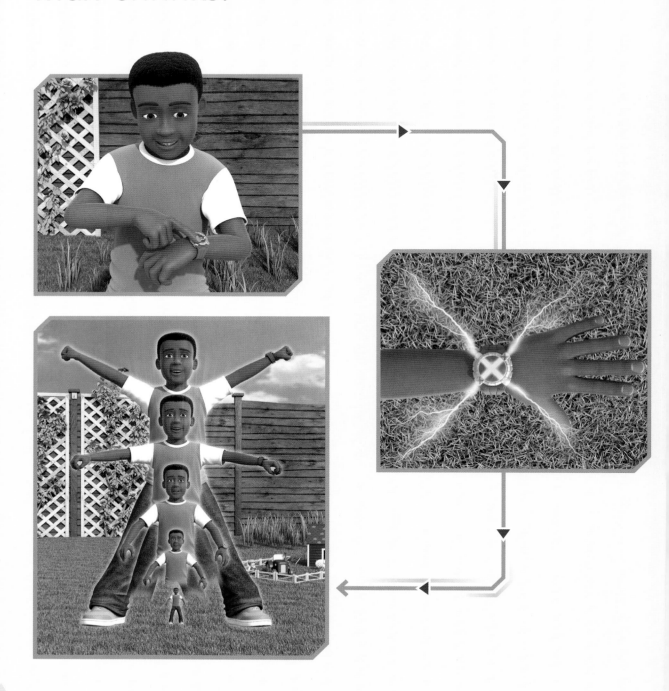

Max sees Nok.
He asks him to help look for
the cow.

Nok points to a snail.

Nok points to an ant.

Then Nok hears a buzzing in the air.

They run into the long grass.

Run faster!

The bee buzzes off.

Nok points.
It is the lost cow!

Max puts the cow back on
the farm.

Molly has her cow back.
She is not sad now.

Retell the story

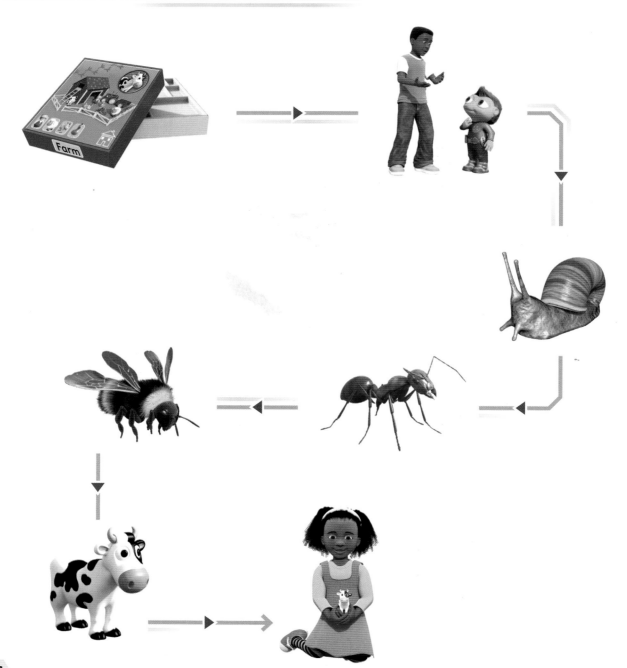